The path leads the way to a seat flanked by twin though different borders of cool colours.

DESIGNING WITH PLANTS

The aim is to create a harmonious border by marrying good structure with contrasts of colour and texture in flower and foliage.

Flowers are what you first think of, but a border should look good when not in flower. Plants with good form and foliage need to be planned for first.

Evergreen shrubs provide a good background to flowers and give solidity to the border. Balance these with flowering shrubs and bold clumps of perennials with architectural merit. Vary the size and shape of these plants contrasting low growing horizontal subjects with rounded forms and the occasional vertical emphasis.

A sunny border composed of golden kniphofia and coral alstroemeria.

These structural plants are permanent and the space allocated to them needs to accommodate their eventual size. The best way to determine their positions is to plot them on a plan of the border drawn to scale.

Herbaceous plants look best planted in bold clumps and drifts. Although tall plants will generally be planted at the back and short at the front a more interesting picture will be created by bringing the occasional tall plant forward and allowing some short ground-covering plants to flow backwards into the border. Choose flowers of varying form and texture.

As well as grading by size you may wish to grade by colour. Pale colours are easier to blend and harmonize than bright ones. Subtle contrasts of colour and changes of tone can build up to the vivid hues. Flower gardens rarely clash badly but orange-reds need to be kept away from blue-reds. This can be done by separating them with green or silver foliage or pale creamy flowers.

Penstemon is an invaluable plant.

Good foliage is an essential ingredient of a successful border. Green and silver leaves will link the flowering plants and enhance them. Look for contrast in habit, size and texture when choosing foliage. Brightly variegated and red foliage is useful used sparingly.

Good plant associations can lift a border from good to excellent. Try to give every plant the best neighbour you can find for it. Look at associations that please you in other gardens and magazines: you will notice that contrasts of form, texture and colour will have been used. Beware, however, of too much contrast or the planting will appear restless. Calm and stability can be imposed on a border by repeating a good plant at regular intervals to unite the whole.

THE TIME-SCALE OF A BORDER

A border when planted is not like a finished painting. In time, growth will alter the scale of plants. In a mixed border the structural framework of evergreens and deciduous shrubs will take about five years to reach reasonable maturity. They must

Allium aflatunense is one of the most ornamental onions.

be given space at planting time to reach this potential. By all means fill the spaces between them with other plants but in the knowledge that some of these will be overwhelmed by the shrubs as they mature.

The planting is not finite. Plants do not always grow as you expect them to, so be prepared to move them around the border the following season. Our taste changes, as does fashion in plants, so always consider replacing a plant that no longer gives you pleasure.

No border is ever perfect but we can have great fun introducing new ideas in our attempt to make it so.

1. MIXED BORDERS

The COTTAGE GARDEN

A cottage garden border in summer. Sweet peas
climbing on a wig-wam of hazel poles are
surrounded by an informal planting of
typical cottage garden plants: perennial
delphiniums and lupins and
annual cornflowers and marigolds.
The path is edged with pinks,
chives and strawberries.

LUPINS, DELPHINIUMS AND HOLLYHOCKS
– such are the cottager's flowers,
underplanted with tulips, anemones,
primroses and violets. Around them
are self-seeding aquilegias, forget-me-
nots, foxgloves and easily grown
shrubs such as philadelphus or
forsythia with gooseberry and
blackcurrant bushes. Roses, clematis,
honeysuckle and sweet peas complete
the picture.

Delphiniums Large-flowered hybrids for early summer. ○, 2.4 × 1m/8 × 3ft

◆ *The stately spikes require discreet staking.*

***Rosa* 'Tuscany Superb'** An old Gallica rose of velvety, dark, blackish crimson, flowering in midsummer. 1 × 1m/3 × 3ft

Alcea rosea Hollyhocks look and grow best in a wall border in full sun. Many colours. 2m × 60cm/6 × 2ft

Lupins are early summer perennials in a wide range of colours and easily seed-raised. ○, 1.2m × 60cm/ 4 × 2ft

Philadelphus coronarius Midsummer flowering shrub. Creamy white flowers. Powerful fragrance. 2.4 × 2m/8 × 6ft

***Syringa vulgaris* 'Alba'** White form of common lilac, highly scented flowers in early summer. 3 × 2.4m/10 × 8ft

HERBACEOUS PERENNIALS

THESE PLANTS ARE THE MAINSTAY of the mixed border from spring until autumn. They die to the ground in winter and re-emerge in spring. They establish quickly, flowering well in their first year.

Persicaria bistorta **'Superba'** (syn. *Polygonum*) Self-supporting pink spikes for a long season in summer. ○, 60 × 60cm/ 2 × 2ft

Achillea millifolium **'Lilac Beauty'** Flowers from midsummer until autumn. Attractive feathery foliage. ○, 1m × 60cm/3 × 2ft

Digitalis ferruginea A perennial foxglove with slender architectural spikes of an unusual shade. ●, 1m × 30cm/3 × 1ft

Campanula persicifolia Nodding blue or white bells in summer. Will seed about discreetly. ○, 1m × 30cm/ 3 × 1ft

A mixed border in early summer. Perennials inter-laced with blue forget-me-nots are planted against a back-drop of yellow-leaved shrubs. Deep blue aquilegias and yellow Welsh poppies (*Meconopsis cambrica*) merge prettily together.

FOLIAGE

AN ABUNDANCE OF HEALTHY GREEN
FOLIAGE will enhance the appearance
of flowers. Red, silver and variegated
leaves are useful but need to be used
with discretion. Look for contrast in
size, shape and texture of leaf.

Symphytum × *uplandicum* **'Variegatum'** Stunning cream
variegated foliage for shade. Cut down the lilac spikes after
they have flowered. Any plain green leaves that develop
should be removed. ●, 1m × 60cm/3 × 2ft

Geranium renardii has pretty purple-veined white flowers, but grow it for its lovely textured foliage. ○, 30 × 30cm/1 × 1ft

Alchemilla mollis Downy, soft green, veined leaves. Frothy yellow green flowers. 45 × 45cm/1½ × 1½ft

Hosta sieboldiana grown principally for its big, textured leaves has cool white flowers. 1 × 1.5m/3 × 5ft

◆ *Requires moisture and some shade. Beware of slugs.*

EVERGREEN SHRUBS

EVERGREEN SHRUBS give a permanent
structure to a border at all seasons
and provide an excellent background
for flowering plants. Conifers,
particularly those of fastigiate or
prostrate habit, can be useful but
restrict yourself to one or two.

Brachyglottis 'Sunshine'
(syn. *Senecio*) Silver leaved
shrub for a sunny well-
drained spot. Yellow
flowers. ○, 1.2 × 2m/4 × 6ft

◆ *A blue clematis looks
good growing through this
shrub.*

Hebe rakaiensis This apple-
green rounded shrub is
outstanding in the dull days
of winter ○, 1 × 1.2m/
3 × 4ft

Eucalyptus gunnii grown as
a shrub by pruning
annually in late spring.

***Euonymus fortunei* 'Silver Queen'** Creamy white variegation. 1 × 1.5m/3 × 5ft

The very dark green of ***Taxus baccata***, the common yew, gives a permanency to this border and makes an excellent background for bright perennials.

◆ *The narrowly upright Irish yew,* Taxus baccata *'Fastigiata', is useful for imposing formality on a border.*

FLOWERING SHRUBS

FLAMBOYANT FLOWERING SHRUBS often
have a very short flowering period.
When choosing them always consider
how they will look when not in flower:
elegance of habit and attractive foliage
are important. Include some with scent
to fill your garden with perfume.

Magnolia × *loebneri*
'Leonard Messel' A
narrow elegant tree 4.5 ×
2.4m/15 × 8ft

◆ *Winter attraction of
branch pattern and buds.*

Buddleja crispa A summer-long succession of orange-throated lilac flowers. Beautiful felted leaves. ○, 2.4 × 2.4m/8 × 8ft

Ceanothus **'Puget Blue'** Neat-textured evergreen foliage. Blue flowers in early summer. ○, E, 1.5 × 2.4m/5 × 8ft

Choisya ternata Glossy green leaves compliment the scented white flowers of Mexican orange blossom. ○, E, 2 × 2m/6 × 6ft

Daphne × burkwoodii **'Somerset'** Variegated, sweetly scented, white-throated pink flowers in spring. ○, 1.5 × 1m/5 × 3ft

Chaenomeles speciosa **'Nivalis' (Flowering quince)** Flowers over a long period in early spring. 1.5 × 1.5m/5 × 5ft

ROSES

OLD ROSES BLOOM EFFUSIVELY, looking and smelling wonderful in early summer. Look also for roses with a longer or repeated flowering period and those with other attributes such as good foliage, nice hips or interesting thorns. A climbing rose on a wall or up a pole will add another dimension.

An association of roses with a complementary planting of perennials. *Rosa glauca*, a vigorous shrub with handsome purple-grey foliage, has small single cerise flowers (not shown) followed by red autumnal hips. The double pink, fragrant flowers of **'Mary Rose'** are produced throughout the rose season on a sturdy bush. *Geranium endressii* and *Viola cornuta* complete the picture.

Geranium 'Johnson's Blue'
Intense lavender-blue
flowers are lovely planted
with pale yellow roses.
30 × 60cm/1 × 2ft

Artemisia absinthium
'Lambrook Silver' Grown
for its silky, silver foliage.
Highly aromatic. ○, E,
60 × 60cm/2 × 2ft

Salvia officinalis
'Purpurascens' The purple-
leaved form of the shrubby
culinary sage. ○, E,
60cm × 1m/2 × 3ft

Stachys byzantina (syn. *S.
lanata*, Lamb's ears) forms a
carpet of weed-suppressing,
woolly, silver leaves. ○, E,
45 × 30cm/1½ × 1ft

Geranium sanguineum var.
striatum A lovely pink form
of the bloody cranesbill,
flowering for many weeks.
○, 30 × 45cm/1 × 1½ft

◆ *More flowers are
induced by cutting back
mid-season.*

FLOWERS *to plant with* ROSES

FLOWERS IN SHADES of pink, purple, lilac, white and creamy yellow associate well with the pinks, whites and crimsons of the old roses. Campanulas, violas and hardy geraniums are excellent companion plants. The brighter tones of modern roses are best complemented by using flowers of similar but softer hues, toned down with cool silver and green foliage.

A harmonious mixed border of roses and other plants. **Rosa complicata**, which has large bright-pink single flowers with white and yellow centres, is here associated with white foxgloves and the blue form of **Campanula persicifolia**, the peach-leaved bell flower.

VERY SMALL BEDS

IT IS OFTEN BEST to treat a very small bed in a formal manner and confine the planting to neat low growing plants with attractive foliage: an edging of box always looks good. Seasonal interest can be introduced with bulbs and bedding plants. In this way changes can be made each year.

This bed is box-edged but here the box is clipped tightly into balls to frame a specimen plant of **Yucca gloriosa** '**Variegata**'.

◆ *Box is easily grown from cuttings so it need not be expensive if you are patient.*

A Winter Border

A VERY SATISFYING BORDER can be made with winter-flowering shrubs, trees with interesting bark, evergreens, early-flowering perennials and bulbs.

***Salix alba vitellina* 'Britzensis'** A willow with glowing orange-red bark on coppiced stems.
1.5 × 1.5m/5 × 5ft

Hamamelis × intermedia A witch-hazel with fragrant yellow spidery flowers on bare branches. Acid soil,
2.4 × 3m/8 × 10ft

Cyclamen coum Brave little pink or white flowers for many weeks which defy the frost. 10 × 15cm/4 × 6in

Galanthus nivalis Aptly named the harbingers of spring, snowdrops are easy to grow, appreciating some shade. 15 × 15cm/6 × 6in

2. SUNNY BEDS AND BORDERS

HOT, DRY BORDERS

ON A SANDY OR STONY SOIL, rain drains through very quickly taking nutrients with it. If the garden is on a slope facing the sun it will be very dry indeed. However, this is exactly what some plants demand: many silver-leaved plants will only thrive in such conditions.

The plants in this very hot, dry, sunny spot have been well-chosen and are obviously thriving. *Cistus* 'Peggy Sammons', penstemon and a graceful dierama are enhanced by silver-leaved shrubs.

◆ *The pots contain purple sage, lavender and a tender aeonium.*

A Sᴜɴɴʏ Wᴀʟʟ

Tʜᴇ ʙᴏʀᴅᴇʀ at the foot of a sunny wall
will be very hot on a summer afternoon.
Choose plants that enjoy a baking.

Abutilon megapotamicum A graceful wall shrub in flower for the entire summer.
◯, 3 × 3m/10 × 10ft

◆ *This is a tender plant but worth trying in a sunny, sheltered corner.*

The seat invites you to bide awhile amongst the fragrant **Madonna lilies (*Lilium candidum*)**. The scented climbing rose **'Golden Showers'** and *Solanum crispum* **'Glasnevin'** flower for many weeks.

***Agapanthus* Headbourne Hybrids** A very hardy strain of the blue African lily.
◯, 60 × 45cm/2 × 1½ft

GRAVEL BORDERS

A GRAVEL BORDER adjacent to a terrace
or drive makes an interesting and
harmonious link to a lawn. Plants that
need good drainage will thrive in this
environment. Site in full sun, excavate
15–20cm/6–8in of soil and replace
with small limestone chippings.

A gravel terrace bed in
early summer with pinks,
campanulas, diascias and a
carpet of pink and white
Thymus serpyllum.

◆ *The pot is planted with*
sempervivums
(houseleeks). The
evergreen rosettes change
colour with the seasons.

Calamintha nepeta Dainty
ice-blue flowers produced
usefully in late summer.
Aromatic foliage.
45 × 60cm/18 × 24in

**Dianthus 'Waithman's
Beauty'** A distinctly
marked, single, old-
fashioned pink; it revels in
a hot gravelly site.
E, 15 × 23cm/6 × 9in

Armeria maritima (Thrift)
From a mat of grass-like
leaves arise little stiff-
stemmed, round flowers. ○,
E, 10 × 20cm/4 × 8in

Campanula poscharskyana
A spreading carpeter for
gravel but not for small
beds. 15cm/6in × indefinite

Pulsatilla vulgaris The
flowers of the Pasque flower
are followed by beautiful
feathery seed heads. ○,
30 × 30cm/1 × 1ft

◆ *There are lovely white,
red, pink and pale
lavender forms.*

Gentiana sino-ornata An autumn-flowering gentian demanding moist, acid soil in sun. 7.5 × 23cm/3 × 9in

Ramonda myconi is an ideal plant for the shady side of a peat-block wall. ●, E, 7.5 × 15cm/3 × 6in

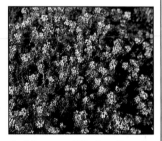

***Aethionema* 'Warley Rose'** A neat little semi-evergreen shrub covered in pink flowers in early summer. ○, 15 × 23cm/6 × 9in

Crepis incana Pink dandelion flowers are seen at their best in a raised bed. ○, 20 × 45cm/8in × 1½ft

◆ *It does not seed about like a dandelion.*

RAISED BEDS

A BORDER ON TOP OF A TERRACED WALL in a sloping garden, or a raised island bed in an otherwise flat garden adds another dimension in design. Small alpine plants are better appreciated nearer the eye and can be provided with the soil and conditions appropriate to their special needs.

A raised bed made with railway sleepers. *Erysimum* 'Bowles Mauve', helianthemums, saxifrages, pinks and the strikingly variegated *Sisyrinchium striatum* 'Aunt May' jostle happily together.

◆ *All sorts of materials can be used to build retaining walls. Brick and stone are traditional.*

3. SHADY BEDS

A SHADY WALL

The climbing **Hydrangea anomala** ssp. **petiolaris** flowers in early summer and reveals its interesting bark and habit in winter. The huge, shiny, tropical-looking leaves of **Fatsia japonica** belie the hardiness of this evergreen shrub. Hostas are at their happiest in shade and ferns revel in such conditions. A dainty form of the lady fern contrasts with the more robust evergreen soft shield fern. A little variegated strawberry weaves about the border.

Planting *under* Trees

FEW PLANTS WILL THRIVE in the dense, dry shade of large mature trees but ivy in its many forms grows well to form a dense attractive ground-cover. Smaller deciduous garden trees allow more adventurous planting in their lighter shade. Violets, hellebores and many of the small spring bulbs do well, flowering as they do before the trees come into leaf.

Convallaria majalis Lily-of-the-valley grown for its delicious scent in spring. 20 × 20cm/8 × 8in

◆ *Lovely to pick for the house.*

Anemone nemerosa
'Robinsoniana' A cool
lavender-blue wood-
anemone flowering in late
spring. Naturalizes well.
15 × 30cm/6in × 1ft

◆ *'Vestal' is a beautiful
anemone-centred double white
form.*

Iris foetidissima Large seed
pods on the Gladwin iris
open to reveal bright
orange seeds in winter. E,
45 × 60cm/1½ × 2ft

Lilium martagon var. *album*
The easily grown white
form of Turk's cap lily.
1.2m × 30cm/4 × 1ft

Symphytum **'Hidcote Blue'**
A vigorous colonizing
comfrey suited to use as
ground-cover. 45 × 60cm/
1½ × 2ft

MOIST BEDS *in* SEMI-SHADE

MOIST SHADE IS A RARE COMMODITY but at the bottom of a slope on heavy soil or alongside a pond you may have it. It can be created artificially with a porous hose laid on or below the surface connected to a water supply.

Dodecatheon meadia f. ***album*** A hardy little shooting star with pendant flowers having reflexed petals. 20 × 15cm/8 × 6in

Primula pulverulenta The colloquial name is candelabra primula. Shades of dark pink, pink and white harmonize beautifully. 60 × 45cm/2 × 1ft

Brunnera macrophylla pulmonarioides Forget-me-not flowers over bold green foliage. 45 × 60cm/1½ × 2ft

***Corydalis flexuosa* 'Père David'** Dainty fern-like foliage above which dance clear blue spurred flowers. 30 × 30cm/1 × 1ft

Mertensia virginica Graceful trumpet-flowers in spring dangle above blue-green foliage that dies down in summer. 60 × 45cm/ 2 × 1½ft

Trollius europaeus Incurved globe flowers of cool lemon yellow over good foliage for early summer. 60 × 45cm/ 2 × 1½ft

The feathery flowers and foliage of astilbe are the perfect foil for the bold-leaved hosta.

◆ *Plants requiring similar conditions frequently look good together.*

4. PLANTER'S PALETTE

PASTELS

A border of pink and lilac flowers looks charming in the soft light of late summer and autumn. This group of late-flowering perennials will be in bloom for many weeks. *Anemone* **'September Charm'** with its simple, pink flowers and the elegant bright lavender-blue spikes of *Perovskia atriplicifolia* are complemented by the filigree silver leaves of *Artemisia* **'Powis Castle'**. Cyclamen and low-growing asters are in the foreground.

BRIGHT YELLOWS

YELLOW IS CHEERFUL and attracts attention. It is enhanced by good green foliage and a few white flowers. The bright shades of yellow harmonise with the hot oranges and orange-reds of late summer to make a very bright border. Year-long interest can be achieved by planting shrubs with yellow or variegated leaves.

Euonymus **'Emerald 'n' Gold'** and *Cedrus deodara* **'Golden Horizon'** provide year-long colour and form. A cut-leaved, golden elder adds summer interest.

◆ *Annual poached-egg plant* (Limnanthes douglasii) *and perennial* Corydalis lutea *complete the picture.*

Iris pallida **'Variegata'**
retains the beauty of its
leaves throughout the
summer. ○, 45 × 30cm/
1½ × 1ft

Valeriana phu **'Aurea'** Eye-
catching bright yellow
leaves for early spring. ○,
20 × 30cm/8in × 1ft

Euphorbia polychroma bursts into flower in late spring with
a long-lasting display of yellow and green bracts. 45 ×
60cm/1½ × 2ft

◆ *Forget-me-nots (myosotis) are a lovely combination with this
euphorbia,*

HOT REDS

BRIGHT RED IS EYE-CATCHING and appears to bring the border nearer to the viewer. In a small garden this can make the garden itself feel smaller. Planted with bright green foliage the red will seem even brighter. A more subtle effect is achieved by using harmonizing foliage in tones of brown, black and purple.

Crocosmia **'Lucifer'** A magnificent tall crocosmia whose sword-like leaves retain their good looks throughout the summer. 1.2m × 30cm/4 × 1ft

◆ *Divide this vigorous plant in spring if it becomes congested.*

***Cordyline australis*
'Purpurea'** A temporary
tender addition to a border
for the summer. ◯, E,
1m × 60cm/3 × 2ft

***Dahlia* 'Bishop of
Llandaff'** The flowers are
in perfect harmony with the
bronze foliage.
75 × 45cm/2½ × 1½ft

***Penstemon* 'Red Knight'**
Encourage repeat flowering
by cutting out stems that
have finished flowering. ◯,
E, 75 × 45cm/2½ × 1½ft

***Euphorbia dulcis*
'Chameleon'** Brownish
purple leaves of summer
turn orange-red in autumn.
E, 40 × 40cm/16 × 16in

***Tulipa* 'Apeldoorn'** A
vigorous, very hardy tulip of
eye-dazzling red. Nice with
cream wallflowers.
60 × 20cm/2ft × 8in

COOL WHITES

WHITE FLOWERS AND GREEN FOLIAGE
look sophisticated and are particularly
good in the formal planting of
geometric beds. White shows up well
in a shady corner and in the evening.
A large border planted entirely in
white needs a dash of one other
colour to enliven it: soft apricot or
pale blue works well.

Campanula latiloba alba A
bell-flower seen at its best
in partial shade.
1.2m × 30cm/4 × 1ft

◆ *Handsome evergreen
basal leaves are a winter
bonus.*

Lilium regale The regal lily is easily grown, given good drainage and sun.
1.2m × 30cm/4 × 1ft

◆ *This midsummer lily is powerfully scented.*

A beautiful single white **peony**, **'White Wings'**, is the star of this early summer border. It is seen against a background of ***Crambe cordifolia*** with its haze of tiny flowers. The use of pale apricot **foxgloves** with white avoids the blandness of an entirely white border. White **aquilegias** and ***Viola cornuta alba*** complete a tranquil composition.

5. FILLING THE GAPS IN BORDERS

ANNUALS *and* BIENNIALS

THESE PLANTS are easily grown from seed and are useful for filling large gaps in new borders. Annuals flower in their first year and biennials in their second.

Salvia sclarea var. **turkestanica** A dominant biennial with big hairy leaves and lavender-purple bracts. 75 × 30cm/2½ × 1ft

Myosotis alpestris There are also pink and white forms of the forget-me-not. 30 × 30cm/1 × 1ft

Limnanthes douglasii The poached-egg plant is a good front row annual for a sunny spot. 15 × 15cm/ 6 × 6in

Cheiranthus cheiri Grow wallflowers as biennials. Good mixers with all spring bulbs. 45 × 30cm/1½ × 1ft

HALF-HARDY PERENNIALS

THESE PLANTS make a valuable contribution to the summer border, flowering with abundance all season long. They are not winter-hardy so need to be propagated from cuttings every year.

Cosmos atrosanguineus A curiosity: dark reddish-brown flowers smelling of chocolate. ◯, 60 × 45cm/ 2 × 1½ft

Heliotropium peruvianum Plant this beside a seat on the terrace where its scent can be appreciated. 60 × 60cm/2 × 2ft

Felicia amelloides A wonderful clear blue, yellow-centred daisy. ◯, 45 × 45cm/1½ × 1½ft

Solanum rantonnetii makes a sizeable free-flowering shrub in one year from cuttings. ◯, 1.5 × 1.2m/ 5 × 4ft

***Arctotis* × *hybrida* 'Apricot'**
Red, white and yellow
African daisies are good for
'hot' summer beds. ○,
45 × 30cm/1½ × 1ft

Use pelargoniums
(commonly known as
geraniums) in shades that
are sympathetic to their
bed-fellows.

***Osteospermum* 'Buttermilk'**
Cool pale yellow petals
fading towards the dark
centre are unusual. ○,
60 × 30cm/2 × 1ft

Sphaeralcea munroana
makes a mat of foliage
covered in flowers all
summer. *S. fendleri* is a paler
pink. ○, 30cm × 1m/1 × 3ft

***Argyranthemum*
'Vancouver'** Paris daisies or
marguerites have pink,
white or yellow, single or
double daisies. ○, 1 × 1m/
3 × 3ft

BULBS *and* TUBERS

BULBS add an element of surprise in a border: they appear when we have forgotten that we have planted them! Hardy bulbs such as daffodils are left in the soil and multiply. Tender subjects such as dahlias and gladioli will need to be lifted in autumn.

Tulipa **'Purissima'** Perfect with yellow polyanthus and good dark green foliage. ○, 40 × 20cm/16 × 8in

Gladiolus byzantinus An early gladiolus that can be left in the ground. The later gladioli are not hardy. ○, 60 × 15cm/2ft × 6in

Narcissus **'Rip van Winkle'** A tough little double daffodil, perfect for a raised bed. It multiplies rapidly. 15 × 15cm/6 × 6in

Fritillaria imperialis A stately spring bulb for good well-drained soil in sun or partial shade. Crown imperials have a ring of orange, red or yellow flowers on tall leafy stems, crowned with a tuft of leaves. The bulbs should be planted on their sides with some coarse sand. 1.5m × 30cm/5 × 1ft

CLIMBERS

CLIMBING PLANTS are generally grown on a wall or fence at the back of the border or up a pole or obelisk to add height. Less formally they can be used to scramble into established shrubs or allowed to sprawl forwards to cover the dying foliage of earlier flowers.

Clematis × *durandii* has a very long flowering season. Lovely scrambling through *Brachyglottis* 'Sunshine'. 1.5 × 1.5m/5 × 5ft

Eccremocarpus scaber A long succession of red, yellow or orange flowers for full sun. Easy to grow from seed which is produced in abundance. 3m/10ft

Humulus lupulus **'Aureus'** A wonderful, yellow-leaved form of hop making vigorous sprawling annual growth. In a small garden confine it to a pole. 4m/13ft

Lathyrus rotundifolius The Persian everlasting pea has early summer flowers of an unusual shade of soft brick red. 2m/6ft

Plants *in* Pots

Unexpected gaps in borders can be
filled with plants kept in reserve in pots:
lilies and hostas are excellent for this
purpose. The pots give added height.
In a formal setting large terracotta pots
will reinforce the formality and can be
replanted seasonally.

A shallow pot, planted with
silver saxifrages, has been
raised on a plinth to give it
more importance.

This very formal border alongside a shady path uses
repetition of identically planted urns to achieve unity.
Hedera helix **'Parsley Crested'** is the ivy used.
Spilling across the path are *Hosta* **'Thomas
Hogg'** and *Alchemilla mollis*. The ivy will
look good at all seasons but will be
the dominant feature in winter
when the herbaceous
plants are dormant.

Index of Plants